Presented To

_____

By

_____

Date

_____

THE
POCKET DEVOTIONAL
for MOTHERS

Honor Books
Colorado Springs, Colorado

The Pocket Devotional for Mothers
ISBN 1-56292-875-9

Copyright © 2002 by Honor Books, Inc.
4050 Lee Vance View
Colorado Springs, CO 80918

Compiled and written by Angie Kiesling

Introduction

Mothers are the original multitaskers. With so much to do, they spend most days doing two or three things at once. Sound familiar? So how can you grow spiritually in the middle of this maelstrom of activity? *The Pocket Devotional for Mothers* can teach you biblical principles of living and mothering—and it can teach you *on the run*.

Each selection provides a brief scripture, pertinent quotation and a short reflection to help you apply the biblical principle. This conveniently-sized devotional goes with you in a purse, a diaper bag, or even a glove compartment in a car for moms who spend their days chauffeuring children to activities. The devotions are short enough that a wait in the doctor's office or soccer practice can provide that key moment in the day to restore your frazzled spirit and reset your energy level to full.

The Pocket Devotional for Mothers will transform your life through regular time with God, even if you are on the run. This book will run with you and keep you running for Him and for your loved ones.

Motherhood is a partnership with God.

For this child I prayed; and the
LORD hath given me my petition
which I asked of him; Therefore
also I have lent him to the
LORD; as long as he liveth
he shall be lent to the LORD.

1 SAMUEL 1:27-28 KJV

Free On-the-Job Training

Being a mother is demanding, draining, rewarding, and high-risk. We come to the task unprepared, then find ourselves enrolled in a rigorous on-the-job training program that spans two decades. Over the course of those years, we get more than we bargained for: tears enough to last a lifetime, but joy that outweighs the sorrow; regret for the things we did wrong, but memories we'll carry all the way into Heaven.

Though babies aren't born with instructions, God is a faithful partner in our work. Like the silent partner in a business, He's always in the background, providing wisdom when we need it and emotional solvency we can bank on.

Motherhood is a strenuous job indeed, but when we approach it with God holding our hand, the trip is worth the taking. Best of all, it transforms us into someone we never dreamed we could be.

Good mothers, like professional athletes,
make the job look easy.

All that I am or hope to be,
I owe to my mother.

Get all the advice you can and
be wise the rest of your life.

PROVERBS 19:20 TLB

8

A Chance to Mold

Mothers are a lot like sculptors. They start with an unmolded child and through hard work and attention to detail, help shape that child into the masterpiece God wants him to be. It's been said of sculpting that the chunks of marble that are chipped away are just as important as the stone that remains. When the art is complete, the artist will be able to appreciate the pieces that fell to the floor by seeing the beauty of the masterpiece. After all, it takes careful craftsmanship to choose what goes and what stays. Both are required for any creative process.

As a mother, you've been given the divine call to mold a life. Stop and think about it. That's a staggering responsibility. God entrusted to you the child or children you've received because no one else could do the job quite like you!

When you're molding children, keep a steady hand and a seeking heart.

Beautiful as seemed
mama's face, it became
incomparably more lovely
when she smiled, and
seemed to enliven
everything about her.

*The joy of the LORD
is your strength.*

NEHEMIAH 8:10

Mom? . . . Ma?— Hey! You with the Apron!

The memory of a mother's sweet face bent over her young child with eyes full of love is one of life's richest treasures. Those who carry such a memory are thankful; those who don't, long for it. Mothers touch us at a primitive level. A loving look, a soft lap, a voice singing lullabies—these are the things that stay with us throughout our lives, whether we're consciously aware of them or not. That early nurturing leaves traces on our souls, shaping us into the people we become.

What will your children remember about you? Will they recall frequent hugs and words of encouragement, or will the word *mother* conjure up images of someone too busy to notice the little things? Will they recall your smiling face, your laughter? Or the harsh words you lobbed at them?

For them let the word *mother* be synonymous with *love*.

Take time to make memories with your children.

A mother is a person
who sees that there
are only four pieces of pie
for five persons and
promptly remarks that
she's never cared for pie.

"*It is more blessed to
give than to receive.*"

ACTS 20:35

Mother's Heart— No Batteries Required

No other role in life stretches us, grows us, and empties us of ourselves like motherhood. It turns a selfish person into a selfless person. Why? Because the love we bear for our children is the closest we ever come to mirroring true *agape* love—the God-kind of love. With the birth of each child comes a love we didn't know we possessed. Along with that love comes the desire to give ourselves wholeheartedly to our tiny, helpless creations—our children.

What gift can you give your child today? Think beyond the material to those intangible gifts that mean so much: your time—play a game with your toddler, your attention—help your middle-schooler with homework, your warm embrace—no child is too old to hug. When it comes to love, remember that quantity counts as much as quality.

A mother's heart is like an Energizer battery— it's keeps giving and giving and giving.

A man's work is from
sun to sun, but a mother's
work is never done.

*Her candle goeth not
out by night.*

PROVERBS 31:18 KJV

Pulling an All-Nighter

A mother's day starts early and ends late; sometimes, in those years when her children are very young, it even stretches through the night. We've all seen sleep-deprived mothers of newborns who manage to keep going despite the lack of energy. Knowledge of their babies' needs is fuel enough to help them go the distance.

The mother instinct lasts a lifetime, answering the call to tend, nurture, mend, or heal—all at a moment's notice. Remember the woman of Proverbs 31, whose "candle goeth not out by night"? That word picture paints an accurate portrait of the mother who puts her children before herself, meeting their needs before her own. All night long, she is attuned to her household like a hen brooding over her chicks.

Though a mother's job is never-ending, once you start the journey of motherhood, you're hooked—no other role in life is quite so fulfilling to a woman.

Once you're a mother, you're a mother always.

What he greatly thought,
he nobly dared.

As he thinketh in his heart,
so is he.

PROVERBS 23:7 KJV

Ignite an Inspiration

Let the story of your children's lives be called *Great Expectations*. What you inspire them to do— believe them capable of doing—has a remarkable way of coming true. These self-fulfilling prophecies seem to work their way outward from deep inside, where the true self resides. The children who are told, "You'll never amount to anything," frequently grow into stunted adults, never achieving their full potential. But the children who grow up hearing words like "You can do it!" probably will.

Never underestimate the power of your words in your children's lives. Though they may not realize it for years, they look to you for inspiration and identification. Who they are now—and the people they are becoming— mirrors what they glean from you. Like unconscious harvesters, they pick up the mannerisms, attitudes, and expectations you sow into their lives today.

Make this day count.

Children who learn to light candles
will never curse the darkness.

They who have steeped
their souls in prayer, can
every anguish calmly bear.

Devote yourselves to prayer,
keeping alert in it with
an attitude of thanksgiving.

COLOSSIANS 4:2 NASB

Praying by Example

As the saying goes, "There's no such thing as atheists in foxholes." Sooner or later, prayer finds us if we haven't already discovered it. And what an advantage we have if we grew up with a praying mother! Children taught to pray by their mothers get a head start in life by that early introduction to God. Even simple rhyming prayers like "Now I lay me down to sleep . . ." can lay a foundation for God-seeking later in life. But the sooner we cultivate the habit of prayer, the better.

Children come into the world wide-eyed and full of wonder. They listen to our stories about God and find Him wholly believable and imminently real. Untarnished from life, they find it easy to imagine a great King who lives in the sky and loves them as a Father.

Don't wait till later—introduce your children to God at an early age.

A praying mother is Heaven's biggest ally.

Words are things, and a small drop of ink Falling like dew upon a thought, produces That which makes thousands perhaps millions think.

She opens her mouth in skillful and godly Wisdom, and on her tongue is the law of kindness [giving counsel and instruction].

PROVERBS 31:26 AMP

Words that Echo

Words are like arrows: they shoot from our mouths and often find their target. When we strike a bulls-eye, that target is changed by the marks we leave. What kind of mark do your words leave on those around you—especially your children? Could it be said of you that you always find the good in people, as well as in circumstances? Do you look for ways to build up rather than tear down by the words of your mouth? Are you as quick to repeat the positive as you are the negative?

It's true that kind words cost little but they pay lifelong dividends. Their echoes resonate across the decades and span any distance. Your children will remember what you said to them long after they've flown from your nest. Make it a point to feather that nest with loving words and kind deeds while you have the chance.

Watch your words, and
they'll reward you someday.

The most useless day
of all is that in which
we have not laughed.

There is a right time for
everything . . . A time to laugh.

ECCLESIASTES 3:1-4 TLB

Take Two and Call Me in the Morning

If you don't have a keen sense of humor already, you'll quickly develop one as you watch your child grow and develop. The alternative is to go raving mad! God must have known we'd be tested and tried on a daily basis—and just as often find ourselves in need of the good medicine of laughter. Children are natural clowns and see the funny in everything. When we allow ourselves to see through their colorful eyes, we catch that childlike humor like the flu.

If you haven't stopped to watch your children at play lately, take the time to do so. See how they interact with other children, or their toys, and note how often they laugh. The simple joy of living lights their eyes, and their vivid imaginations—untainted by a world-weariness—find the wonder in everything. Life is a something to marvel at when seen through childlike eyes.

Laugh with your children; it'll do you good.

The purest affection
the heart can hold,
is the honest love of
a nine-year-old.

*Let us hold fast the profession
of our faith without wavering.*

HEBREWS 10:23 KJV

It's Elementary, Dear Watson!

We strive after wisdom but seldom measure up to the gut-level awareness that children possess. But since you're a mother, nobody has to tell you this—you experience it day after day with your own offspring. Those young minds are attuned with razor-sharp clarity to your true feelings. They can read your face better than Sherlock Holmes reads a clue.

Maybe God gifted children with this built-in lie detector for our own good. We train them, correct them, and guide them, but in the end our children help to keep *us* honest. Unsettling, you say? You'd better believe it. But it's also a blessing in disguise. Thank God every time your children catch you in a half-truth. Thank God that, because your life is on display, you're much more careful about how you live. With His help, your children will keep you on the straight and narrow.

Be mindful how you live—
your children are watching!

You cannot teach a child to take care of himself unless you will let him try to take care of himself. He will make mistakes; and out of those mistakes will come wisdom.

"My prayer is not that you take them out of the world but that you protect them from the evil one."

JOHN 17:15

The School of Hard Knocks Is Enrolling

There's nothing like the school of hard knocks to teach us—and our kids—the stuff that's worth knowing in life. Remember the first time you reached out to touch the inside of a hot oven door? Chances are good you didn't do it again. Or how about the time you tried to jam a dime into the gumball machine and discovered that you got neither the gumball nor your dime in return. The next time, you probably took much more care in how you wiggled that precious dime into place.

When we overprotect our children, trying to keep them from every hurt and heartache, we do them a disservice. Experience is the best teacher, and the sooner they learn that, the better. Be there to guide them and pass along the wisdom you've gleaned in life. But don't be surprised when they have to find out for themselves.

Shield your children from danger,
not experience.

Just as the tree is bent,
the tree is inclined.

We have different gifts,
according to the grace given us.

ROMANS 12:6

Free Gift Enclosed

At birth God gives each child a beautifully wrapped present before sending that child into the world. Inside are all the talents and abilities unique to that individual, stored up for eventual use. Some children open their packages and find the gift of music. Others uncover a gift for creativity. One child's package may contain athletic ability; another may not realize the hidden gift until young adulthood.

As a mother, you can help cultivate your children's talents by being a keen observer. Watch them while they play at a young age. What do they gravitate toward most often? What activity makes your son or daughter happiest? Later, in school, notice in which subjects they excel. If your expectations for your children lie outside their giftedness, try adjusting your dreams so that the thing they love is also the occupation they flourish in someday.

Dream big dreams for your children,
and your enthusiasm will be contagious.

Remembered joys
are never past.

The memory of the righteous
will be a blessing.

PROVERBS 10:7

Remember When the Baby Spit Up On . . .

Among life's most valuable treasures, memories rank high. The funny thing is we often don't realize the moments we're living in right now will be the memories we look back on one day. It takes the perspective of time—dosed with a touch of nostalgia—to appreciate memories. But with a little retraining of the mind, you can learn to see every moment as a future memory. A good place to start is with your children.

Motherhood is ripe with the potential for lots of memory making. Each day ask God to give you eyes that see beyond your frustrations to the fleeting treasure that day represents. Your children will never be this *exact* age again. Freeze the moment in time through your memory. Fill your memory storehouse to overflowing. Someday you'll want to take those dear memories out and look over them like a box of old photographs.

Memories made with love outlive all others.

He too serves a certain
purpose who only
stands and cheers.

*We have around us many people
whose lives tell us what faith
means. So let us run the race
that is before us and never give up.*

HEBREWS 12:1 NCV

Still Fit into Your Cheerleading Outfit?

Popular culture says your children should act, dress, look, speak, and think a certain way. Peer pressure hems them in, trying to squeeze them into the accepted mold. But you, as a mother, are a far more vital influence over your children's lives. Despite media messages to the contrary, parents carry the fiery torch that leads the way for their children to follow. What they see you do, they will one day emulate.

The right to be bold—to stand up and make a difference—is the greatest inspiration you can give your adolescents. Encourage them to swim against the tide if the tide is moving in the wrong direction. Applaud their efforts to uphold what's right, and make sure you lead by example. Though the road through adolescence is rocky, you and your teen will emerge all the stronger if you forge ahead on the Godly path.

Become your teenager's biggest champion in life.

Be not angry that you
cannot make others as
you wish them to be,
since you cannot make
yourself as you wish to be.

*It is better to be slow-tempered
than famous; it is better to have
self-control than to control an army.*

PROVERBS 16:32 TLB

You Can't Find Self-control in the Yellow Pages!

Children bring out the best—and worst—in us: the best because they make us laugh; the worst because they know how to push our hot buttons and demand supernatural patience at times.

It's interesting to note what a high premium God puts on self-control. He rates controlling one's temper over controlling a large army. From the perspective of Heaven, it's better to be a slow-tempered commoner than a best-selling author, star athlete, or renowned actor. Fame is shallow and fleeting compared to the strength of a personality brought under control.

Did your child make you want to scream today? Take comfort in the knowledge that God is on your side, holding your hand as you muddle your way through the mothering maze. Sure, you'll make plenty of mistakes. Every mother does. But you'll also do a lot of things right, with God's help.

Patience grows stronger with regular use. Did your patience get a workout today?

Parents who are afraid
to put their foot down
usually have children
who step on their toes.

*Those who spare the rod hate their
children, but those who love them
are diligent to discipline them.*

PROVERBS 13:24 NRSV

Love Can Be Spelled T-I-M-E-O-U-T

When your own parent said, "This is going to hurt me more than it hurts you," you probably thought, *Yeah . . . right!* But now, as a mother, you know just how true those words can be. Loving parents don't get their kicks by correcting their children, but the alternative is much, much worse. Children who aren't disciplined with a firm, loving hand grow up feeling unloved and unprotected. Paradoxically, the children with boundaries feel safe. Those boundaries are there for a reason, and deep inside they know it, despite their occasional desire to kick at the fence.

Think of your own life. Have you ever done something wrong and felt God's loving but persistent discipline? Just as He promised in His Word, God chastises us as a kind earthly father disciplines his children. Indeed, it's because of God's great love that He is motivated to steer us toward right living.

Love goes hand-in-hand with discipline.

Children have more need
of models than of critics.

*Be very careful, then, how
you live——not as unwise
but as wise.*

EPHESIANS 5:15

Macramé a Kid

Lessons learned early in life have remarkable staying power. The things your parents taught you probably influence your core beliefs and decisions today, all these years later. Like images from your childhood neighborhood, they are an ever-present part of your reality—woven like macramé knots into the fabric of *you*. Even if you've adapted those life lessons to fit your world today, they remain a part of you. Your parents, in a sense, wove their beliefs into you. These leave an indelible mark on the soul.

In the hustle and bustle of life, it's easy to forget how meaningful words and actions are. What you say and do to your children today will produce results in the long haul, not just the short term. If you choose carefully, those words and actions will bear the kind of fruit that God smiles upon. Teach your children, but teach them well.

Let your life be one your children want to emulate.

Our patience will achieve
more than our force.

Ye have need of patience.

HEBREWS 10:36 KJV

Hurry Up and Wait

Did you ever notice how everything in the created world works on a timetable? No amount of coaxing can alter the order of things. If you want to grow corn, you have to sow the seeds and wait for harvest. Fall colors blaze to life only once a year—no matter how often we long to see them. Babies still take nine months to "bake," regardless of advanced medical technology. In short, when dealing with God's created order, it's *hurry up and wait.*

That chicken won't hatch any faster if you turn up the heat—it will die. There is no way to microwave life. But when you allow everything to follow its ordained course and render to everything a season, the rewards are worth the wait.

It's the same way with children. Let them grow at their own pace. Everyone will enjoy the process much more.

Rejoice in God's perfect timing for everything.

There is in all this cold
and hollow world no
fount of deep, strong,
deathless love, save that
within a mother's heart.

Love is patient, love is kind. It
does not envy, it does not boast, it is
not proud . . . Love never fails.

1 CORINTHIANS 13:4-8

When Their Ruffs Turn into Meows

Sooner or later, almost every mother's heart is broken by her children. The wonderful thing about a mother's heart, however, is that it comes with an expandable capacity—able to love even when that love is scoffed or spurned.

For most mothers, the heart-breaking years coincide with the teen years. One article described children as dogs, eager to see you at the end of a day and always full of love. But when they enter the teen years, those dogs become cats, disdainful of your attention and sometimes downright mean. Cats are famous for their independence. If you want them to do something, they'll do the opposite. But the good news, the article said, is that someday—typically in their early twenties—your cats will turn into dogs again. When they do, all your spurned love will come back to you in a full measure!

Love regardless of how you are loved in return.

A good laugh is
sunshine in a house.

*The cheerful heart
has a continual feast.*

PROVERBS 15:15

One Cup Giggles, Two Cups Laughter

Children look forward to coming home when *home* is joyful. Not just your children, but your children's friends will gravitate to your house if it's a happy home. Kids can't be fooled. They pick up tension and strife like radar screens scanning for enemy aircraft. Their sensors are especially attuned to love and warmth, and where these two traits flourish, so do they.

What kind of home do you provide for your family? Is it filled with laughter, peace, and upbeat words? If not, there's always time to change. Why not submit your home to a joy test over the next few weeks. Note how often your kids laugh; look to see what emotions are reflected on their faces. Do they seem eager to come home after school, or are they ready to flee the minute they come in the door?

Fill your home with laughter, and your children will grow a joyful spirit.

Home, sweet home—
where each lives for the
other, and all live for God.

None of us lives to himself alone
and none of us dies to himself
alone. If we live, we live to the
Lord; and if we die, we die to the
Lord. So, whether we live or die,
we belong to the Lord.

ROMANS 14:7-8

Harbor Sweet Harbor

When God invented the family, He created a remarkable institution. More than anything else, families are designed to protect and nurture individual lives. They provide a safe haven—a place where the kindred can be themselves, where they can laugh, cry, dream, experiment, even rant if they have to. The family allows children to learn about themselves and the outside world while still anchored in that safe harbor. Like baby birds snug in a nest, they can peek out at the wide blue sky and prepare for the day when they, too, will launch out into it.

The phrase "home sweet home" is true only if home is a place where you and your children long to be. Make it your goal today to provide not only a safe haven but a sweet haven for your family. The memories you create will be etched with tenderness and lined with love.

Pour your heart into your home.

To weep is to make
less the depth of grief.

He that goeth forth and weepeth,
bearing precious seed, shall
doubtless come again with rejoicing.

PSALM 126:6 KJV

"But while He Was Still a Long Way Off . . ."

Prodigal son stories pull at the heart in a special way. Ask almost any mother of an adult child, and they'll probably have a prodigal son story or two of their own to tell. Often the child who demands the most from us and breaks our heart becomes the one closest to us in later years, after grace and forgiveness have wrought a healing in their hearts and ours. Then we realize the tears we cried and prayers we prayed were not in vain at all. Through the valley of sorrow, we emerge stronger, deeper.

Do you have a child who's breaking your heart? Commit that child daily to God and trust Him to work through your prayers, in His way and His perfect timing. He promised to complete the good work begun in each of us, and that includes prodigals of every age and stripe. It also includes *you*.

Tears are not wasted when they're poured out in love.

Nothing has a better
effect upon children
than praise.

*Anxiety weighs down the human
heart, but a good word cheers it up.*

PROVERBS 12:25 NRSV

Spread Your Word Fertilizer

Roses denied sunshine don't grow well—or don't even grow at all. A tree without water shrivels and dies. Children deprived of praise become depressed and cynical. But children who are showered with genuine praise (not mere flattery) develop a can-do belief in themselves and the goodness of God.

We all need to know we are worthy of being loved and worthy of having our love received in return. Like exotic flowers in a greenhouse, children flourish in a home where love is poured out and encouragement is plentiful. Even newborn babies respond physically to love and nurture, while those denied it often become sickly.

If you do nothing else today, remember that your words contain the power to uplift or tear down. Use them wisely. Be quick to repent when unkind words are used. Your children will thrive under loving care, loving words, a loving touch—spread liberally and frequently.

Make someone glad by what you say today.

The best academy,
a mother's knee.

*Provoke not your children to wrath:
but bring them up in the nurture
and admonition of the Lord.*

EPHESIANS 6:4 KJV

Hug a Kid, Burn a Calorie

Whether they're on your knee for discipline or a bedtime story, children are shaped by those times when they are closest to your heart—literally. Remember how it felt to be held on your mother's lap? Even now those earliest memories are a part of you. Like images seen from your peripheral vision—not clearly in focus but there nonetheless—they follow you through life.

Each day presents a golden opportunity to mold the budding life of your children. If the day calls for discipline, dispense it with love and understanding. Be sure to end the day with your children close to your heart. Read to them. Pray with them. Hold them close. Sing a lullaby until they fall asleep. Someday the sweet memory of these times together will rush up to meet them as they raise children of their own.

Always keep your arms open and your lap available to your children.

A mother understands
what a child does not say.

*The LORD searcheth all hearts,
and understandeth all the
imaginations of the thoughts.*

1 CHRONICLES 28:9 KJV

That Third Eye

Mothers come equipped with a special type of maternal telepathy: no matter what their children are up to, they know it instinctively. Mothers seem able to read minds, confounding even the slyest of their off-spring. When you were young, that mind-boggling mother feature was maddening; now that you're a mother yourself, you probably smile and thank God you possess it too.

The best use of this gift is perhaps the least obvious: not to catch your children in devious activities, but to see into their hearts and really know them. Use your women's intuition to hear what your children are crying out for on the inside. They may not be bold enough to ask out loud. But with God's help, the mother in you will know what they need most and understand how best to offer it. Let your heart be your guide.

Tune in to what your child is not saying today—it will speak volumes.

Great persons are able
to do great kindnesses.

Be kind and compassionate to one
another, forgiving each other, just
as in Christ God forgave you.

 EPHESIANS 4:32

Of Course I'll Share My Last Godiva Chocolate with You

One important task assigned to motherhood is the command to teach your children kindness to others. Kindness is the staple of a well-ordered world. If your children get no other benefit from growing up in your presence, let them be able to look back one day and say, "I learned kindness from my mother."

Kindness has become a rare commodity in today's dog-eat-dog world. Instead of on others, people seem focused on *themselves*—so much so that an entire decade was dubbed the "me generation." We've traveled far from the days when the golden rule was taken at face value and practiced in our culture.

Your children will learn many things in life. Some will come from you, and bits of wisdom will be gleaned through the school of life. But let it be that they will always back and say they learned kindness at home.

Make yours a kinder, gentler home.

The best time to give children your advice is when they are young enough to believe you know what you are talking about.

There is a right time for everything . . . A time to speak up.

ECCLESIASTES 3:1-7 TLB

Please Pass the Obedience and the Creamed Kindness

The passing of wisdom from one generation to the next is like a long daisy chain linked by love. What you learned from your parents, you pass on to your children. They in turn will teach their own children one day, recalling the lessons they learned from you. Decades from now that chain of wisdom will continue to link your descendants one to the other, and you will be an important part of it.

Young hearts are like sponges, soaking up whatever is given them. If children are given love, they learn to love in return. If they are taught obedience, they learn to obey. If they are shown kindness and understanding, they give the same to others. If children are taught to laugh, they grow up happy.

Just for today, ask God for the wisdom to guide your children in the way of righteousness.

Wisdom dwelling in the home is better than material blessings.

If thou shouldst never
see my face again,
Pray for my soul.
More things are
wrought by prayer
Than this world dreams of.

Pray without ceasing.

1 THESSALONIANS 5:17 KJV

Monkey See, Monkey Do

Remember the phrase "monkey see, monkey do"? Children are like that, mimicking their parents' gestures, mannerisms, words, habits—even their tone of voice. We shouldn't be surprised when they pick up a habit we practice with regularity, whether good or bad. After all, we are their constant role models.

A mother who prays gives her children a powerful example of godliness in action. Talking about God is one thing, but talking *to* Him on a daily basis is another thing. If you make prayer a priority in your home, your children will notice it—even if they pretend not to. Pray for them, but also pray with them. The daily ritual of prayer, over time, will be sewn into their lives like a golden thread among denim.

When the time comes for them to leave home and launch out into adulthood, that pattern of prayer will serve them well.

Callused knees make for a Godly home.

A mighty fortress is our God, A bulwark never failing; Our helper, He, amid the flood Of mortal ills prevailing.

"My grace is sufficient for you, for my power is made perfect in weakness."

2 CORINTHIANS 12:9

God's Unlimited Coupon—Grace

Toddlers are living reminders that we can do all things when God is with us! What mother hasn't thrown up her hands in frustration when her child entered the terrible twos? Yet somehow we make it through those years—and live to tell the tale, replete with stories about how adorable our children were at that age. Years down the road, we may even long for those innocent baby days again when our sons or daughters trek through the terrible teens. Suddenly, those terrible-two tantrums seem like a cakewalk by comparison.

The good thing about God's grace is that it's always in abundant supply. God doesn't ration grace like wartime gas coupons. He is always ready to dispense it, just at the moment we need it most.

If today promises to be a rigorous trial, remember that God's promise to carry you through is stronger still.

Grace is ours for the taking each new day.

A child is fed with
milk and praise.

*Let no corrupt communication
proceed out of your mouth, but
that which is good to the use
of edifying, that it may minister
grace unto the hearers.*

EPHESIANS 4:29 KJV

A Steady Diet of Praise

Praise is to the spirit what milk is to the body. Deprive a child of either one, and he will become sickly over time. The best way to grow children who are healthy physically is to feed them nutritious food; the best way to ensure they grow healthy spirits is to sincerely praise them on every occasion.

We all need to know when we've done something wrong, but it's equally important to know when we've done something right—perhaps even *more* important. Like the boss who always complains about a job done wrong, the parent who needles her child for every fault will foster an attitude of deep resentment. Imagine how that child must feel!

Today, take the time to praise your children for something. It might be as simple as how they light up a room with their smile or pick up their toys after they play.

*Keep your heart-pantry stocked
with praise for every occasion.*

I think that saving a little child and bringing him to his own, is a darned sight better than loafing around the throne.

The fruit of the righteous is a tree of life; and he that winneth souls is wise.

PROVERBS 11:30 KJV

Be a Missionary at 123 West Elm Street

Raising a Godly child is perhaps the most significant thing you can do as a mother. That heritage of faith eclipses all other traits—genetic or otherwise—that you could pass down to the next generation.

Trend researchers say that children who grow up in church are more likely to attend when they're adults. Habits learned in childhood have a way of firmly sticking. The habit of seeking God's will for your life can't be transferred to your children, but it can definitely be modeled for them.

As you seek to shine your light in a dark world, remember that your first disciples are those little ones at your knee. Even if your light shines no further than home, you can still go to sleep each night knowing that you spread the Good News. Teach your children to fear the Lord today, and they will follow Him for a lifetime.

Point your children toward God.

You hear that boy
laughing?—you think
he's all the fun; But the
angels laugh, too, at
the good he has done.

*A merry heart doeth
good like a medicine.*

PROVERBS 17:22 KJV

Laugh Your Way into Their Hearts

A home brimming with laughter is always a pleasant place to be. Any recipe for household joy includes a healthy dose of humor, and those who make time for family fun are never disappointed. In fact, why not tickle your child's funny bone every day?

Is your heart in need of good medicine? Laugh with your children today. Go see a funny movie together. Chase butterflies with them in the backyard. Play a wacky board game with them. Once you start laughing together, it will become addictive. Soon you'll look for other opportunities to laugh with your kids.

Try this experiment: Put a "funny pot" in the middle of the kitchen table. Let each member of the household write down ways to have fun. Each morning, have one child pull an idea from the pot—then make sure you do that activity together before bedtime. The giggles you share will be remembered.

Make time to laugh with your children today.

Don't view me with
a critic's eye, But pass
my imperfections by.
Large streams from little
fountains flow, Tall oaks
from little acorns grow.

*Many that are first shall be last;
and the last shall be first.*

MATTHEW 19:30 KJV

Gotta Watch the Quiet Ones

Crack open the biography of any great person, and you'll almost always find a story of humble beginnings. God doesn't require great talent; He only needs a willing vessel—someone who can hear His voice of instruction. Children with teachable spirits are prime candidates for accomplishing God's purposes on Earth. Train your children to seek Him early, and they will be open to their divine destiny. Imagine your joy when you see the Lord's plan for their lives unfolding—knowing that you played a pivotal part in their development.

At the same time, remember that God may accomplish His perfect will for your children without astounding feats by them. They may live a quiet life devoted to Him and still fulfill the destiny He has marked out for them. Often it's those quiet wonders that leave the largest ripple in the pond of time.

God may speak to you through your child today—are you training him to listen?

That government is best
which governs the least,
because its people
discipline themselves.

Even a child is known by
his actions, by whether his
conduct is pure and right.

PROVERBS 20:11

"I Love You— Now Go to Your Room!"

Though they may protest loudly today, your children really do want the boundaries you set for them. Those children without guidelines—free to do as they please—most often feel unloved and uncared for. Guidelines and boundaries are like foul lines on the ball field of life. Players who score within the lines are safe, whereas those who venture outside get called out. For children, being safe in a family means knowing that mom is there and requires certain behavior of them, and expects communication on their part. Consequences follow bad behavior, just as rewards follow good behavior.

Discipline isn't fun for the parents or the children, but is necessary to help children to grow up healthy. They might not appreciate it today, but later in life when they reap the benefits and have children of their own, they'll thank you.

Loving discipline reaps children the world will be proud to call future citizens.

Boundaries equal safety for your children.

I do the very best
I know how,
the very best I can.

In all the work you are doing,
work the best you can.
Work as if you were doing it
for the Lord, not for people.

COLOSSIANS 3:23 NCV

The Perfect Mother Is a Myth

When all is said and done, we can only do our best and no more. For each person that means a different thing. But God knows what abilities He has put inside you—He knows your strengths as well as your limitations. That doesn't excuse you from doing your best, though, because your best is always achievable. Do that, and leave the results to Him.

No mother is perfect; your own mother probably made many mistakes—and you will do the same. But even with your imperfections, God thinks you are the best person for the job—the best person for your children. What a compliment!

Today, ask God to give you the strength and wisdom to do your best at mothering. That's it! When you can lay your head on the pillow each night, knowing you did your best that day, sleep comes easily—and sweetly.

Do your best each day; God will fill in the gaps.

God can't be always
everywhere: and so,
invented Mothers.

*Let your conversation be always
full of grace, seasoned with salt.*

COLOSSIANS 4:6

People Will Remember You as Grace, Even if Your Name Is Sue

Grace—perhaps no other word sums up God's gift to us as well. Grace permeates all of our lives, and sometimes we scarcely notice it. But if it were snatched from us, the memory of grace would be sweeter than anything else in our lives.

For many adult children, the word *mother* is synonymous with grace. Maybe that's because moms remember what it was like to be children, and their sweet, gentle nature responds accordingly. Often it takes a gentle maturity to realize just how precious grace is in a household full of children. But even if your children are young, they will sense its presence at work, though they may not know what to call it.

For your part, if you see a spark of grace in your children, fan that ember into a flame. They, in turn, will pass it on to their children.

Let the grace of God pour into your home like sunshine through windowpanes.

No legacy is so
rich as honesty.

*An honest answer is like
a kiss on the lips.*

PROVERBS 24:26

Try Not to Kiss Any Strangers

Honesty can be costly—sometimes it hurts to tell the truth, but the alternative is even worse. Children who grow up learning the importance of truthfulness dwell in safety; those who learn to lie walk on shifting sand. Like the old saying claims, "Honesty is the best policy," no matter what the situation is—just be sure to speak it in love.

The Book of Proverbs compares an honest answer to a kiss on the lips. That's really saying something. A kiss is one of the highest forms of affection; you don't kiss strangers, do you? No—kisses are reserved for people who mean a great deal to you. They are not given carelessly. Perhaps that's why Solomon compared an honest answer to a kiss. He knew that honesty, even when it hurts, brings satisfaction to the soul in the end.

No lie ever achieved good results. Make the truth your banner, and fly it high every day.

Encourage truthfulness, even when it hurts.

The Constitution only gives
people the right to pursue
happiness. You have
to catch it yourself.

*Be wise: make the most of every
opportunity you have for doing good.*

EPHESIANS 5:15-16 TLB

Children Go, Memories Stay

When our days grow lean and our remaining years run short, memories will be all that's left to us. How we fill in the time between now and then makes all the difference. What kinds of memories are you making right now? Have you stopped to play with your young children, read a book to your school-age child, listened to the puppy love dramas of your dreamy teens?

Memories are like butterflies—beautiful from a distance but hard to catch here and now. Maybe that's because we get nostalgic about the past but forget that the present—this very moment—will be the past someday. That means it's ripe for memory-making!

Don't let today pass by without doing something special with your children, no matter how small. Someday you'll be able to look back and cherish the memory you made today. Best of all, so will your children.

Make a memory with your children today.

Children seldom misquote
you. In fact, they usually
repeat word for word what
you shouldn't have said.

*In everything set them an example
by doing what is good. In your
teaching show integrity, seriousness
and soundness of speech.*

TITUS 2:7-8

"If I Have to Tell You One More Time . . ."

Have you ever heard your own words coming from your child's mouth? If you choose your words carefully, this is a good thing. If not, you're in for a jolt! Every parent can relate to this. It would be funny if the words they said were always innocent, but when you hear unwholesome talk coming from your child, it's time to take a speech checkup of your own.

You've probably heard jokes about people who live with talking birds. They give away secrets and say some shocking things! What's the best way to retrain the bird? Retrain the owner's own mouth.

It's simple. Make your home a place of kind words and affirming talk. If you practice kindness in your speech, it will come back to you through those young mouths. Ask God to keep you mindful of your tongue today, and never forget how powerful your words are.

A careful tongue makes for a happy home.

God incarnate is the end of
fear; and the heart that
realizes that he is in the
midst . . . will be quiet
in the midst of alarm.

When I am afraid,
I will trust in you.

PSALM 56:3

Are You Still Afraid of the Dark?

A strong storm breaks out during the night, casting shadows on the walls and making the house groan and creak. Young children cower under the layers of blankets and cry out for their mothers. When children feel that touch of love—the comforting presence of Mother—peace replaces terror, and love wraps the little ones in safety.

Fear is a natural part of life, but it needn't be a monster out of control in the lives of your children. As you know too well, not just children get frightened. Although we trade bumps in the night for unpaid bills and scary medical tests, fear still stalks us when we move into adulthood. But we don't have to live in constant fear. The psalmist determined to put his trust in God whenever fear brushed close by. God wants you to do the same. Rest in Him.

God is still a strong tower for any who seek Him.

The greatest of faults,
I should say, is to be
conscious of none.

Confess your faults one to another,
and pray one for another,
that ye may be healed.

JAMES 5:16 KJV

"I Admit It! I'm Addicted to Chocolate!"

Some parents think they have to present a stoic front to their children, showing no signs of weakness. They put on masks to show the world, but reveal who they are deep inside only to a trusted few.

Surprisingly, children are comforted to know the real you. They will trust you more when they sense you are being real with them. At the same time, your transparency will set an example for how they should live—displaying their true selves rather than wearing masks.

Spend time with each child today; and be sure to share your silly side, your foibles, your struggles, and your insecurities. Make your home a place where your children feel safe enough to let down their guard, even if it means seeing their bad side now and then. At the same time, don't be afraid to let them see the real you.

Let your kids see the real you.

If it was going to be easy to raise kids, it never would have started with something called labor.

He gives us more grace.

JAMES 4:6

Give Me Grace (and a Strong Cup of Coffee!)

Being a mother brings out resources you never knew you had. One person rendered it like this: "A woman is like a teabag . . . you never know just how strong she is until she gets into hot water." At each stage of motherhood, you may feel as if you need more grace than ever before: first, during the sleepless nights when a newborn baby rules the house; later, when your child enters the terrible twos. Then comes the transition into dizzying adolescence, when your nerves are constantly frayed. Finally, come those turbulent teen years that mark your child's growing independence from you and home.

No matter what stage of mothering you're in, take comfort in the thought that you're in good company—and strong hands. God promises not to leave you comfortless, nor to let you stumble along life's path without a guiding light. With His help, you will make it through.

Pray for grace and expect it!

While faith makes all
things possible, it is love
that makes all things easy.

*Who can find a virtuous woman?
for her price is far above rubies.*

PROVERBS 31:10 KJV

There's Still Time to Be Wonder Woman

For a few short years in this earthly life, we get to be someone's hero. That's the remarkable thing about motherhood. Even if our children never outwardly say so, tucked away their hearts is a word picture called "Mother" with your gentle, loving face on it. When calamity strikes, they will forever think of you, their safe haven of love from life's trouble.

What a delight it is to know we are dependable rocks to our children. They may see our fears and insecurities at times but still witness the strength we gain from seeking and walking with God. The parent who turns to Him for every decision, large or small, paints in broad strokes a picture of faith and love that can't be ignored.

When the time comes for our children to make their own decisions, they will remember our heroic deeds—things like kneeling to pray when we can't see the way.

You are your child's hero today.

Adversity is the diamond
dust heaven polishes
its jewels with.

Don't try to squirm out of your
problems. For when your patience
is finally in full bloom, then you
will be ready for anything, strong
in character, full and complete.

JAMES 1:4 TLB

Diamonds Are a Mom's Best Friend

As mothers, our job is to mold our children, not change them into something or someone they're not. Forcing a child to be what we want them to be is like trying to squeeze toothpaste back into the tube once it's out. And that's a hopeless task!

The wonderful thing about motherhood is that we get to witness diamonds in the rough while they're still charcoal. Time and pressure will work the miracle of metamorphosis on your children, just as they did on you. At times the transition will be difficult, even painful. You will want to rush in and fix things or help your children across their hurdles. Be there for them, but let them unfold into the people they were meant to be. And every step of the way, cheer them on. They will make it, just as you did. Watch them shine!

Your children are diamonds in the rough—
enjoy them while they're still charcoal.

I know—yet my arms are empty,
That fondly folded seven, And
the mother heart within me
Is almost starved for heaven.

*Watch yourselves closely so
that you do not forget the things
your eyes have seen or let them
slip from your heart . . . Teach
them to your children and to
their children after them.*

DEUTERONOMY 4:9

Feather Your Nest

Childhood is a time for flying—for trying wings while mother hovers nearby. But wise mothers know instinctively that their job as flight instructor will come to an end. Motherhood never ends, but those years of basic training come too quickly to a close.

An old Southern rock song said, "Hold on loosely, but don't let go." That's a good motto for mothers of still-growing children. Eventually you'll have to let them go; but when you do, you will simply transition to holding them in your heart—not by the hand.

Baby steps all too soon turn into a walk, then a run. Before you realize it, your children will be grown and leaving the nest. In the years that remain, do your best to feather that nest with love. When they finally fly away, they'll remember the years in your care as among their best.

Hold your children loosely, but love them with all your heart.

The mother's face and voice are the first conscious objects as the infant soul unfolds, and she soon comes to stand in the very place of God to her child.

They will be called oaks of righteousness, a planting of the LORD.

ISAIAH 61:3

Are You Raising an Elm, A Maple, or a Weeping Willow?

Raising children to be men and women of integrity will be one of your greatest mothering achievements. You have direct input into the shaping of young lives—people who will grow up to be the leaders and parents of tomorrow. And just think—God has entrusted you with this all-important job!

Children guided by love and understanding are like sturdy saplings that sprout into hefty oak trees. They may grow within a mundane garden, surrounded by commonplace shrubs, but when they reach their full height, they will cast enough shade to protect all the other plants in the garden. A full-grown oak tree is a mini-ecosystem, supporting wildlife, providing shade, shelter, and creating beauty in the landscape.

Start today by instilling God's Word into your children. And as you sow integrity into their spirits, you become the gardener of a mighty oak tree of the future.

Children are like acorns that grow into mighty oak trees.

Three things never come again
. . . Never to the bow that bends
comes the arrow that it sends.
Never comes the chance that
passed, That one moment was
its last. Never shall thy spoken
word Be again unsaid, unheard.

*Reckless words pierce like
a sword, but the tongue of
the wise brings healing.*

PROVERBS 12:18

Have Some Salt with Your Morning Tea

Any mother knows that God is a God of irony. Why else would He allow the tiny beings we spawned to catch us in our own inconsistencies? It doesn't take a rocket scientist to figure out there's a divine justice in the world of motherhood.

The place where you are most vulnerable before your children is your mouth—the words you speak. Speak recklessly, and you will pierce their souls and cast a bad example; speak words of healing, and your children will gravitate toward you and speak words of grace. After all, everyone loves to be around those who affirm.

Before you rush into this day, pray for wisdom, and ask God to season your words with salt. Keep watch over your mouth; be a guardian of what you say. Your character will show up in the kinds of people your children turn out to be.

Let your words be seasoned with salt.

Upon our children—
how they are taught—
rests the fate, or fortune,
of tomorrow's world.

*Having done everything . . .
stand firm.*

EPHESIANS 6:13 NRSV

Hold On, Let Go

When Mom or Dad taught you how to ride a bicycle, first they ran along beside you, holding the wobbly bike as you pedaled cautiously. But soon came that horrible moment when they let go—horrible, yet wonderful, because suddenly you found yourself riding alone. You may have taken a tumble or two, but eventually you did it. You were riding a bicycle! It was the most exhilarating thing in the world.

That's how it is with your children. They long to be protected, yet want to gain independence too. A wise parent finds the balance between nurturing and setting free. Sure, you run along beside them during the early years, but the day will come when they strike out on their own—and look back at you with triumphant smiles. Give them your blessing and wave them on. You will have helped to bring adults into the world.

Remember that you're raising tomorrow's adults.

Respect the child.
Be not too much his
parent. Trespass not
on his solitude.

The LORD is compassionate
and gracious, slow to anger,
abounding in love.

PSALM 103:8

Rubber Band Your Children

Motherhood is a curious combination of loving and letting go, of feeding and weaning, of holding on and pushing off the little ones entrusted to us. As you raise your children, there will come times when they pull away from you. Let them. It's like the young bird trying his wings. In order to try them, he has to push away from his mother. Otherwise, his wings wouldn't be his own—and no child wants that.

When your children need time and space away from you, it's just their way of saying, "I want to grow up—but I won't go too far." Like a rubber band that stretches to its fullest range, they'll snap back when they've had enough of solo flight for the time being. Eventually, they'll make the leap out of the nest completely, and on that day you will be glad you taught them to fly well.

*Weave respect for independence
into your actions.*

At the touch of love,
everyone becomes a poet.

May the Lord make your love
increase and overflow for each
other and for everyone else.

1 THESSALONIANS 3:12

Have You Hugged Your Child Lately?

A happy childhood is laced with affection, and hugs are one of the staples of a healthy family. God gave us arms not just for carrying grocery bags, but to wrap around those we love, and our children are at the top of the list. Our affection is an extension of God's love for them.

A hug is a reminder that you think someone is special. It tells them they are worthy of being loved—and not just loved, but touched tenderly. Have you ever seen children who are deprived of affection? When human beings are deprived of love, they grow insecure or mean—and sometimes both. A child who grows up in a house full of love—a home where love is demonstrated daily—puts down solid roots that sustain when life gets rough.

Today, love your children with your arms as well as your heart.

Hug your children like you mean it.

You have confidence
in yourself, which is
a valuable, if not an
indispensable quality.

*Faith is being sure of
what we hope for and certain
of what we do not see.*

HEBREWS 11:1

Put On Your Lipstick, and Let Them See You Smile!

Raising confident children begins with being a confident person yourself. Children are like mirrors, reflecting what they see in you. Arrogance is a trait few admire, but confidence is respected by everyone. Let your children see your quiet confidence as you look to the Lord for wisdom to tackle each new day. Let them see you on your knees when you don't know the answers. That's not a sign of weakness—it's a sign of meekness.

Confidence grounded in faith is stronger than mere confidence alone. Suddenly the God of the universe underwrites your confidence—and His checks never bounce! Teach your children to place their trust in God, despite the odds and outward circumstances. As they seek His face, He will reveal Himself to them and grow their faith as surely as He grows yours. With the Lord's help, you can raise confident kids, confidently!

Confident kids are made, not broken.

The joys of parents
are secret, and so are
their griefs and fears.

*He knows the secrets
of the heart.*

PSALM 44:21 NRSV

One Minute You're Laughing, the Next You're Crying

Some things are too precious for words. Like Mary, we may ponder these things in our hearts but never tell a soul just what they mean to us. Be assured that God knows. He sees your secret joys, as well as your sorrows and fears. He knows the pain and pleasure that go hand in hand with motherhood. But He also makes sure the bittersweet memories stay fixed in your mind and hone your soul. You are changed irrevocably by being a mother. And He stands behind those changes.

A mother's heart is a deep well of emotion. No other job in life brings such intense emotions to the surface, but isn't it worth the effort? Aren't you glad you said yes to the invitation? The experience develops a heart filled with His love and His patience.

Thank God for the joys and the sorrows of motherhood.

Thank God for the gift of motherhood today.

The soul is healed by being with children.

Sing to him a new song; play skillfully, and shout for joy.

PSALM 33:3

Children Ooze Life, Joy, (and a Few Unmentionables)

Whenever you're in need of a spiritual boost, try this experiment: Take your children to a nursing home, and let them interact with the residents. Watch what happens. Sad faces light up, eyes dance, and laughter replaces depression when young children are around. Or visit the playground with your kids in tow. Don't just watch from the sidelines, but play with them. Find out what a seesaw feels like again. Swing high on the swing set. Hold your toddler on your lap and zoom down the slide together. Dig for treasures in the sandbox with them.

Children are a constant reminder that God wants the world to continue. These fresh human beings, still malleable clay, look to us for direction, but we look to them for inspiration—and recaptured innocence.

Be like the psalmist today: sing and shout like a child to the Lord!

Your child's playful spirit can be contagious—try to catch it!

To be blind in the eye
is better than to be
blind in the heart.

*I pray that your hearts will be
flooded with light so that you
can see something of the future
he has called you to share.*

EPHESIANS 1:18 TLB

Broken Toys and Scabby Knees

True treasures are priceless and can't be bought with money. Mothers learn this powerful truth the day they first bring a child into the world. Thereafter, their lives are changed forever—and they become stewards of God's greatest treasures on Earth.

As mothers we get to help shape the souls of our children. No higher privilege could be ours in this lifetime. Indeed, that's a daunting thought. Yet we shoulder the task willingly because love is poured into the daily routine of training our children.

When parenting is done in tandem with God's wisdom, you begin to see with new eyes—eyes that see into the invisible world, not just the world of broken toys and scabby knees. Suddenly you see your children as the men and women they will become, the human beings you are helping to shape for all eternity. You see the awesome partnership between a mother and God.

Judge with the heart, not with the eyes.

Our greatest glory is not in never failing but in rising up every time we fail.

Do not gloat over me, my enemy! Though I have fallen, I will rise. Though I sit in darkness, the LORD will be my light.

MICAH 7:8

I've Fallen and I Don't Want to Get Up!

We all learn by doing. We crawl before we walk and walk before we run—and sometimes we fall down. Falling isn't the important thing. It's what we do when we're down that counts. Do we stay on the ground and give up or brush off our knees and keep going? Get up and go!

Emerson had the right idea. Like most achievers, he knew that victory only comes to those who get in the game. Setbacks are part of life; they're intended to thwart us but can actually make us stronger. Like a football player with the ball, we may get tackled—may even fall down—but if we get up and rush toward the goal, we will be winners in the end.

Keep your own God-given destiny in mind as you go through today. Set your mind on the goal and you will achieve it.

If you fall, get up and get going!

O what a happy soul am I!
Although I cannot see, I am
resolved that in this world
Contented I will be; How many
blessings I enjoy That other people
don't! To weep and sigh because
I'm blind, I cannot, and I won't.

I have learned, in whatsoever state
I am, therewith to be content . . .
I can do all things through Christ
which strengtheneth me.

PHILIPPIANS 4:11-13 KJV

Being Thankful for Elastic Waistbands!

Some days we feel like a small hamster on the eternal wheel, mindlessly going through the same routine. Mercifully, God knew we'd have days like that and promised to carry us through when we come to the end of ourselves. Sometimes it's only when we come to the end of ourselves that He displays His mighty power in our lives.

Although tedious routines can wear you down, they are also a perfect place in which to learn contentment. Yes, that dreaded C word that the apostle Paul tossed out so easily. The truth is, contentment is easier spelled than achieved, but we start the process toward contentment by counting our blessings.

Make a list of everything you are thankful for. Be specific: hot water, good friends, grocery stores, long-distance phone calls, healthy children—everything you can think of. When you've compiled your list, you'll be that much closer to contentment.

Contentment leads to a happy heart.

Smile and feel ten years
younger; worry and
get gray hair.

"Don't be anxious about tomorrow.
God will take care of your tomorrow
too. Live one day at a time."

MATTHEW 6:34 TLB

The Sun Will Come Out Tomorrow

If we live in the future, we'll miss the present—and it's here in the present that tomorrow's memories are made. Don't miss out! Your children will never be this very age again, never look this way again. Each day they are changing and getting older, and you'll never recapture the moments that drop into your lap today.

The remarkable thing about God is that He is Lord of the future as well as the present. He already knows what lies ahead for you and your children, and He is preparing you even now. With God keeping watch on the future, you are free to enjoy the present and throw your worries out the window. They won't help the situation anyway.

As your children see you trust God about tomorrow, they will follow your example. Let quiet confidence replace your worries today, and God will take care of your tomorrows.

Treasure all your todays.
Tomorrow will come soon enough.

To instill a healthy prayer
life in your children,
pray yourself.

Evening, and morning, and at noon,
will I pray, and cry aloud:
and he shall hear my voice.

PSALM 55:17 KJV

Is Prayer Your 9-1-1?

When Susanna Wesley, mother of Charles and John—along with seventeen other children—needed privacy to pray, she simply pulled her apron over her head and thus entered her prayer closet. Her children might have snickered at first to see their mother cloaked by an apron, but over time their amusement must have turned to awe, even respect. Any mother who is desperate enough for God to seek Him amid the clamor of a busy household is an unforgettable role model to her children.

Prayer is either a habit or an emergency response in people's lives. How much better it will be if you teach your children to pray not just in emergencies, but in all things, every day, even if it is just to commune with God.

Bedtime and mealtime prayers are wonderful traditions in a Godly home, but go one step further and train your children to pray without ceasing.

*Pray not just for your children
but with your children.*

Most troubles are imaginary: what you think are huge clouds in the sky may be nothing more than dust on your eyelashes.

Cast your cares on the LORD and he will sustain you; he will never let the righteous fall.

PSALM 55:22

Take Your Worries for a Walk

Thankfully, most of what we worry about never comes to pass! Instead, God's promise to provide comes true in the nick of time, or we are spared some calamity that we fretted over for months. Even when we do walk through the valley of the shadow of death, He is there holding us firmly by the hand.

The moment you become a mother, a new set of concerns is dropped in your lap. Suddenly you worry about things you never dreamed of before. But along with those concerns comes the love to face up to them— or the grace to turn them over to God.

No one lives a trouble-free life, but the life lived in step with God walks on a higher plane. He won't shield you from all your troubles; He merely promises to make you a better person from having faced them.

Get the best of your worries;
don't let them get the best of you.

To show a child what
once delighted you, to
find the child's delight
added to your own,
this is happiness.

*A happy heart makes
the face cheerful.*

PROVERBS 15:13

"Wow, Mom, I Thought You Were Like One Hundred Years Old!"

It's time for the family vacation. Instead of a theme park, you take the kids to your hometown and show them the places where you played as a child—the tire swing your dad hung from the huge oak tree in the backyard, the woods that transformed into a magical kingdom long ago, the vacant lot where you skinned your knees and formed lifelong friendships, the pool where you first learned to swim.

As you tell the story of your childhood, you see your children's eyes widen in wonder—and the moment is priceless. Sharing secret joys with your children is a wonderful way to foster the mother-child bond. What better way to link with them than through the eyes of the child deep inside you?

Let the wonder of life fill you with awe today. That sparkle in your eyes will speak volumes to your children.

Fan the flames of childlike
wonder in your heart.

Kindness, nobler ever
than revenge.

*Those who are kind reward
themselves, but the cruel
do themselves harm.*

PROVERBS 11:17 NRSV

Small Kindnesses

Kindness toward others begins in the home. Whatever your children see you do, they will replicate in their own lives. Let them see you love others through your words and deeds. Allow them to overhear you complimenting the clerk at a convenience store, greeting the mailman, cheering on a friend in need.

Children know what it's like to be bullied in the school yard or picked on by a so-called friend. They learn early that pretty is as pretty does. Though the lesson may be hard-won, it's usually those who bear the brunt of cruelty who develop the greatest capacity of compassion toward the brokenhearted—and esteem kindness all the more.

Today, seek ways to teach your children about small kindnesses. Opening the door for a stranger or letting someone else have the first drink at the water fountain may not earn brownie points, but it will create a big heart.

Keep the golden rule alive in your household.

Let thy child's first lesson
be obedience, and
the second will be
what thou wilt.

*Whoever loves discipline loves
knowledge, but he who hates
correction is stupid.*

PROVERBS 12:1

Ouch!

Now, here's a thought that cuts against the grain of popular culture: if you want to grow smarter, embrace discipline. If you want to gain knowledge, learn to love correction. Imagine that! Once again God proves the paradox of His ways—the rugged route that leads to life and walked only by a few.

Children don't lap up correction like kittens do milk, but the sooner they learn to expect it, the sooner they will grow wise from it. What's the first rule of every agreeable household? According to Ben Franklin, it's obedience. Once that lesson is snugly intact, everything else falls into place.

When it comes to discipline, we're not so different from our children. We don't relish the thought of spending time in God's woodshed, nor do we enjoy the pain discipline brings. But the results that come from being disciplined by our Father are priceless.

A teachable spirit is a valuable thing to God.

The future is as bright as
the promises of God.

*The path of the righteous is
like the first gleam of dawn,
shining ever brighter till
the full light of day.*

PROVERBS 4:18

On a Journey with God

Time rattles onward, never stopping to let us reflect too long on where we've been—usually we are too concerned with where we are going. And though we each have the same twenty-four hours in every day and the same 365 days in a year, the years seem to go by faster the older we get.

Do you remember how time stretched out in an endless ribbon when you were a child? That's what it looks like to your children today. Their perspective is narrower than yours. That's why they need your insight and wisdom to guide them. At the same time, instill in your children a sense of excitement about what the future holds. They need not fear the future when trusting in God. Together, the three of you will make the journey go well—until that day when you stand back and let them go on, hand in hand with their Maker.

Enjoy the journey today as you walk
with God and your children.

God will not demand more
from you as a parent than
what He will help you do.

*With God nothing
shall be impossible.*

LUKE 1:37 KJV

A Secret Partner

It's a comfort to know we don't have to parent alone. Even if you're a single mom, you have an unseen Partner helping you through each day. He may not always be obvious to your senses, but He's there nonetheless—holding you up when you can't take any more and whispering wisdom in your ear when you might otherwise despair.

God not only makes Himself available, He longs to be a part of your daily life. Often we simply forget to ask. What is impossible for us is more than possible for the God who created the universe.

Is there a task overwhelming you today? Do the walls seem to be pressing in on you? Cry out to God, and He will come to your side. He will either remove the obstacles, or He will walk through the rocky places with you—carrying you when you can go no further alone.

*When the going gets rough,
the wise start praying.*

The art of motherhood
involves much silent,
unobtrusive self-denial,
an hourly devotion which
finds no detail too minute.

*Now faith, hope, and love
abide, these three; and the
greatest of these is love.*

1 CORINTHIANS 13:13 NRSV

Divine Motherhood

Any mother would agree—once her baby is born, her heart is forever on the line. Remarkably, it's a love she willingly gives, a reckless abandon to love another, even if they forsake her in the process.

Being a mother requires faith, hope, and love—faith to carry you through when parenting gets tough, hope that your children will turn out right, and love to last a lifetime. Armed with those three, you can face the monumental task of raising children with confidence.

The hard times will come, but the tall mountaintops will overshadow the dark valleys and make you glad you took the trip. Someday when you are old, you will be able to look back on your life and say, "The best thing I ever did was become a mother." At the very least, motherhood is a divine lesson in loving others.

Let love be your legacy.

These lovely lamps, these
windows of the soul.

*Her children arise and
call her blessed; her husband
also, and he praises her.*

PROVERBS 31:28

Blue, Brown, or Hazel, Babies Love 'Em

Even if your childhood memories are faint, you can probably still remember your mother's eyes. No other facial feature conveys love the way eyes do, and a mother's eyes—when filled with love and understanding—are an awesome thing to behold. They watch carefully from the playground bench as her children swing high into the air. They watch, brimming with tears, as her children sing a solo in the school play or score the winning point. Those same eyes look at the child who is terrified from a loud storm—and convey love, comfort, and protection.

No wonder even newborn babies seek the face of this person called "Mother." That very first eye contact forms a lasting bond, a rock of safety, for the child. And at the same time, it tethers a mother's soul permanently to her baby.

Be the kind of mother whose eyes reflect a loving soul, whose children call her "blessed."

Give the look of love to your children.

Teach us, good Lord, to serve thee as thou deservest; To give and not to count the cost; To fight and not to heed the wounds; To toil and not to seek for rest; To labor and not to ask for any reward, Save that of knowing that we do thy will. Amen.

I bear on my body the marks of Jesus.

GALATIANS 6:17

War Wounds

Suppose you have a rose garden. One day you decide that your child is old enough to tend it. So you send him out with the pruning shears, and he heads into the garden. You hear him cry out the first time a thorn sneaks through the glove. He runs back to you and shows you the wound, but you show him the thorn-pricks on your own hands. Then you point to the vase of red roses on the table. "It hurt a little, but they were worth it," you say.

Later he is showing off the roses and the bandaged wounds with pride.

Sometimes the tasks of life bring us in the way of small hurts and fatigue. Nothing worthwhile comes without a price. We need to teach our children to forge ahead in challenging activities in spite of sore muscles or lost television programs.

Teach your children that the cost of service is a badge of honor.

You are the bow from
which your children,
as living arrows,
are sent forth.

*I have no greater joy than this,
to hear that my children
are walking in the truth.*

3 JOHN 4 NRSV

Shoot Them toward the Straight and Narrow

Make the way straight for your children, and someday they will follow. When walking through deep snow, it's always easier to step in the footprints of the person up ahead. The tracks they leave behind make the path manageable, although it still requires some effort on the part of those who follow. That's how God intended mothers to guide their children. All children must take their own steps on the journey, but their steps are nestled into the larger prints the mom-boots leave behind.

Like an archer's bow, you are the instrument that will propel your children into the world. How you fit them into the bowstring makes all the difference. A loose fitting will result in a wayward arrow; a taut fitting will cause the arrow to strike true.

Raise your children so that they strike true. It's always a joy to hear that your children are walking in the truth.

Shoot straight so that your children might also.

Mother's arms are made
of tenderness, and sweet
sleep blesses the child
who lies therein.

As one whom his mother
comforteth, so will I comfort you.

ISAIAH 66:13 KJV

Dr. Mom

Moms have a special way of doctoring bruised knees and hurting fingers. Band-Aids and antiseptic play a part, of course, but the real healing begins the moment she kisses the wound and makes it all better. No one can mend a bruised heart the way a mother can, either. When her children come home crying, she is there to soothe their pains, rock away their childish fears, and apply love lavishly.

The best part of motherhood is the daily offering of unconditional love. Who would have thought that giving our hearts away would be such a joy! But ask any mother, and she'll most likely agree: comforting children is a divine destiny, a privilege not to be taken lightly.

As you go about your day, think of all the ways you can bring comfort to your household. Save enough love for each child, no matter what the day brings.

There's no love like a mother's love.

Motherhood is, after all,
woman's great and
incomparable work.

For this reason a man will leave
his father and mother and be
united to his wife, and they
will become one flesh.

GENESIS 2:24

Independent Ironies

Life is full of paradoxes. Consider this one: We allow our children to lean on us so that one day they will be able to stand alone. Odd, isn't it? We raise our children just to let them go. We nurture them for years, then push them out of the nest at the proper time.

From the day our children arrive, we teach them independence—moment by moment, one step at a time. Each day they are growing away from us. They may cling at first, but eventually every child experiences the rapture of self-discovery and then, later, independence.

Inside this truth is another paradox: The more we mature, the more God designed us to depend upon Him. Even when our children learn to walk alone, they walk best in step with the Almighty. The final equation resembles something like this: Dependence upon parents equals independence; dependence upon God equals blessing.

*Teach your children to fly
from you and cling to Him.*

Mother is the name
for God in the lips and
hearts of little children.

The LORD said to him, "This is
the land I promised on oath to
Abraham, Isaac and Jacob . . . I
have let you see it with your eyes,
but you will not cross over into it."

DEUTERONOMY 34:4

A Trip for One

A mother's task is similar to that of Moses as she prepares her children for the journey of life. She leads them through the wilderness, settles disputes, pleads to God on their behalf, and finally stands at the crest of the hill, shading her eyes and looking out at the place they will go. She is not able to go there with them, however. That part of the journey all children must make own their own—following God for themselves, not because their Mother requires it.

Those who start down the path with God beside them find the way much easier and the burden much lighter. Just as Moses did, guide your children as far as you are allowed to go. Teach them the commands of God, and then leave the rest to Him. With such a start in life, they will go far in their spiritual walk.

Raise your children in such a way that they complete the story of your life.

Wisdom is that
apprehension of heavenly
things to which the spirit
rises through love.

*If any of you lack wisdom, let him
ask of God, that giveth to all men
liberally, and upbraideth not;
and it shall be given him.*

JAMES 1:5 KJV

When We Were Young and Sleep Deprived

Most of us would admit to being scared out of our wits when we took our first baby home from the hospital. We were packed on our way with a smile and a wish for the best—but had no idea what to do beyond the obvious. If the baby cries, feed him. If the baby dirties a diaper, change it. If the baby cries, burp him—or is that a hungry cry? Yikes!

Though we may smile at the memory, we all bumbled a bit during those early days when every gesture our sweet babies made was a marvel, a thing of great wonder. Remarkably, God placed a mothering instinct inside us that springs into action when the action is called for. As we go along, somehow we learn just what to do at every stage of growth and to call on Him.

Wisdom is ours for the taking when we ask God to give it.

The hand that rocks
the cradle is the hand
that rules the world.

*Teach a child to choose the right
path, and when he is older,
he will remain upon it.*

PROVERBS 22:6 TLB

Not a Homeschooler? Think Again!

For twelve years we send our kids to school, cramming their heads full of knowledge. But only at home can they learn the really useful stuff—the things that comprise the shaping of a life. What good is math if a child never learns to divide right from wrong? What use is biology if a child never learns to revere the One who spoke all life into being? What purpose is reading if a child is never introduced to the written Word of God?

Though school shapes the mind, a mother's task is to shape the heart and steer the spirit toward the divine. God will do the rest. It is our job as mothers to start our children down the straight and narrow. If we do that faithfully, He will see to it that their feet remain steadfast years down the road.

Every mother "homeschools" her children.
What can you teach yours today?

Because I feel that, in the
Heavens above, The angels,
whispering to one another,
Can find, among their burning
terms of love, None so
devotional as that of "Mother,"
Therefore by that dear name
I long have called you.

You reap whatever you sow.

GALATIANS 6:7 NRSV

A Lifelong Job

Who can put a price tag on a mother's worth? Of all the jobs in life, this one probably holds the highest honor in God's eyes. Anytime you start to feel insignificant, stop and think: you are shaping *lives!* You have been given the responsibility of molding human beings! Their outcome will be determined largely by what you do—or don't do—right. If that's not reason enough to take the task seriously, what is?

Motherhood is a lifelong calling. Long after your children are grown and gone, you will still hold them in your heart, just as you did the moment you first looked into their newborn eyes. Can any other ambition in life measure up to this one?

Take a moment today to thank God for your children—not just for who they are, but for the awesome privilege of being the one they call "Mother."

No other title means so much as "Mother."

Reason to rule but
mercy to forgive:
The first is the law,
the last prerogative.

Mercy triumphs over judgment.

JAMES 2:13 NASB

Mercy Served in Generous Portions Here

The grace and mercy of God are unfathomable. Thank God for His gift of mercy! As the apostle said, it triumphs over judgment. In that one statement, we are able to wipe out the image of a stern, justice-dispensing Ruler who watches from Heaven—waiting for us to slip up. In its place emerges a picture of the Good Shepherd, who lovingly pursues the one straying sheep, who writes in the sand rather than condemning a woman caught in sin, who dines with carousers so that He might point them toward a better way.

Just as you received mercy, be merciful to those in your life—especially your children. The value of mercy far outweighs the importance of learning earthly alphabets and traditions of men. It paints symbols and pictures. That's why even the youngest children can grasp its meaning and respond in kind. If they see mercy given, they will give mercy too.

Put mercy on the menu of your life every day.

Who ran to help me when
I fell, And would some
pretty story tell, Or kiss the
place to make it well?
My mother.

See how very much our heavenly
Father loves us, for he allows
us to be called his children—
think of it—and we really are!

1 JOHN 3:1 TLB

Gather Them in Your Arms

You lose your child in a large department store, so you run to the service desk and wait frantically for that familiar face to appear. Minutes drag by like hours. You pray—plead—with God. Then you see a small figure break through the crowd. A smile lights up the child's face while rushing into your arms. *My beloved child,* you think as you gather the little one into your arms.

Mother love is the closest we'll ever come on Earth to grasping what God feels for us. In that moment of cherishing, when your child is safe once again in your arms, a rush of warmth and protectiveness washes over you, and you glimpse the divine. It's only through the dark moments that we come to appreciate the light. And when the light finally breaks through, after the valley of shadow, it shines like the midday sun.

Remember that God's love for you is even greater than yours for your children.

Acknowledgements

(6,12,14,58,82,88,90,120,132) Anonymous, (8,74,106) Abraham Lincoln, (10) Leo Tolstoy, (16) Homer, (18) Richard Monckton Milnes, Lord Houghton, (20) Lord Byron, (22) Sébastien Chamfort, (24) Holman Francis Day, (26) Henry Ward Beecher, (28) Alexander Pope, (30) James Montgomery, (32) Henry Adams, (34) Thomas à Kempis, (36) Chinese Proverb, (38) Joseph Joubert, (40) Edmond Burke, (42) Felicia Hemans, (44,146) William Makepeace Thackeray, (46) T.J. Bach, (48,78,126) William Shakespeare, (50) Sir Philip Sidney, (52) James Russell Lowell, (54) Jewish Proverb, (56) Miguel de Cervantes, (60) Alfred Lord Tennyson, (62) Martin Luther, (64) Mary Lamb, (66) John Hay, (68) Oliver Wendell Holmes, (70) David Everett, (72) Thomas Jefferson, (76) Sir Edwin Arnold, (80,128) Benjamin Franklin, (84) F.B. Meyer, (86) Thomas Carlyle, (92) Archbishop Robert Leighton, (94) Margaret Elizabeth Sangster, (96) Granville Stanley Hall, (98) Rose Terry Cooke, (100) B.C. Forbes, (102,114) Ralph Waldo Emerson, (104) Plato, (108) Francis Bacon, (110) Fyodor Dostoyevsky, (112) Arabian Proverb, (116) Fanny Crosby, (118,122) Chinese Proverb, (124) J.B. Priestley, (130) William Carey, (134,148) Honoré de Balzac, (136) Guillaume de Salluste, (138) Saint Ignatius of Loyola, (140) Kahlil Gibran, (142) Victor Hugo, (144) Edward Carpenter, (150) William Wallace, (152) Edgar Allan Poe, (154) John Dryden, (156).

References

Unless otherwise indicated, all Scripture quotations are taken from the *Holy Bible, New International Version®* NIV®. Copyright © 1973, 1978, 1984 by International Bible Society. Used by permission of Zondervan Publishing House. All rights reserved.

Scripture quotation marked AMP is taken from *The Amplified Bible, Old Testament.* Copyright © 1965, 1987 by Zondervan Corporation, Grand Rapids, Michigan. Used by permission.

Scripture quotations marked NASB are taken from the *New American Standard Bible.* Copyright © The Lockman Foundation 1960, 1962, 1963, 1968, 1971, 1972, 1973, 1975, 1977, 1995. Used by permission.

Scripture quotations marked KJV are taken from the *King James Version* of the Bible.

Scripture quotations marked NRSV are from the *New Revised Standard Version of the Bible,* copyright © 1989 by The Division of Christian Education of the National Council of the Churches of Christ in the USA. Used by permission. All rights reserved.

Verses marked TLB are taken from *The Living Bible* © 1971 © 1986. Used by permission of Tyndale House Publishers, Inc., Wheaton, Illinois 60189. All rights reserved.

Scriptures marked NCV are quoted from *The Holy Bible, New Century Version,* copyright © 1987, 1988, 1991 by Word Publishing, Dallas, Texas 75039. Used by permission.

Additional copies of this book and other
titles from Honor Books
are available from your local bookstore.

Also available:

The Pocket Devotional
The Pocket Devotional for Women
The Pocket Devotional for Teens

Other Honor Book titles you might enjoy:

Everyday Prayers for Everyday Cares for Mothers
God's Little Devotional Book for Mothers
God's Little Devotional Book for Mothers—
Special Gift Edition
God's Little Devotional Journal for Mothers
God's Little Lessons for Mothers
My Personal Promise Bible for Mothers
Quiet Moments with God for Mothers

If you have enjoyed this book, or if it has impacted
your life, we would like to hear from you.

Please contact us at:

Honor Books
4050 Lee Vance View
Colorado Springs, CO 80918